A CHRISTIAN WRITER'S POSSIBLY USEFUL RUMINATIONS ON A LIFE IN PAGES

ANGELA HUNT

Hunt Haven

Hunt Haven
Press

Visit Angela Hunt's Web site at www.angelahuntbooks.com

ISBN-13: 978-0615873145, 978-1961394759
ebook: 978-1961394766

"What I like in a good author is not what he says, but what he whispers."

-Logan Pearsall Smith, "All Trivia," *Afterthoughts*, 1931

Other Books in the **Writing Lessons from the Front Series**

INTRODUCTION

In 2013, on some unknown day, I moved into my fourth decade of professional writing. The thirty years that lie behind me have been filled with peaks and valleys, pleasure and pain, happiness and heartbreak. I've seen publishers come and go; I've watched editors become agents and editors again. I've seen bookstores disappear and watched as self-publishing—a term that used to emit the stink of desperation—become respectable, profitable, and desirable.

As a writer, my thirty years have been filled with learning, growing, and adjusting. Techniques that were popular thirty years ago (block paragraphs of description, action/reaction sequences) have fallen out of favor, and new techniques have evolved. I've learned the wisdom of flexibility, and that a writer must follow principles, not rules.

I've found writing friends that are closer than brothers and sisters. I've met my share of challenges, and I have not always overcome them. But I've tried to do my best in everything.

Along the way, I have written blog posts, articles, and notes to friends. I've filled notebooks with thoughts and quotes. I've awakened in the middle of the night to jot down a brilliant idea, only to wake in the morning and find that the brilliance vanished with the darkness.

Caveat: because I am a Christian, my faith informs every area of my life, especially my writing life. This does not make me bellicose, belligerent, or dull-witted, but if you are afraid of reading something that might challenge your own set of beliefs, you should probably drop this book immediately. You have been (lovingly) warned.

I believe some of my ruminations might prove useful or entertaining . . . so I have gathered them up and offer them to you, another writer. Remember to do the same for the writers who will come after you in thirty years or so.

--Angela Hunt

CHAPTER ONE

A Life in Pages

I THINK I'VE BEEN DESTINED TO LIVE MY LIFE IN PAGES. AS A kid, I loved to read--not to write, but to read books that carried me away. No one ever told me what *not* to read, so I read pretty much everything I could get my hands on.

Growing up, I always enjoyed English class because of the reading thing, and I vaguely recall trying to write a mystery novel in the seventh grade--I think I still have the few pages somewhere. But it was highly derivative of Nancy Drew, though the main character's name was Jade. Funny how those things stick in your mind.

In high school I took advanced English classes, but I was definitely not the head of the class. Never thought of writing as a career, and in my "Career English" class, we learned more about how to correctly fill out a job application than how to write for a living. Ditto for college--when I changed my major from Vocal Performance to English, I was studying literature, and high-brow lit at that: Shakespeare and Chaucer and 17th Century British poets (that's when I fell in love with John Donne).

After college I decided to become a writer because I wanted a job that allowed me to stay home with my babies . . . so I had to learn the ends and outs from scratch. Ran to the library to gather books for instruction. Didn't go to a writers' conference for years, never joined a critique group—and maybe those were good things. By the time I went to my first conference as a student I'd published eleven books.

I learned all I needed to know from books—formatting, the genre blueprints, the standards of proper professional behavior. How to submit, how to write a query letter, how many pages should be in a picture book. That's why I'm a little baffled today when people think I can tell them how to get published over lunch.

The answers are all in pages. Whenever I had a question, I ran to the library for the answer and found it within the books on the shelves. You can, too, except today you can probably find most of what you need to know on the Internet.

Though none of my novels are strictly autobiographical, all the things I wrestle with end up in my daily pages. There's a certain symmetry to that . . . and I like it.

CHAPTER TWO

Give Me a Story, Please

RECENTLY I WENT THROUGH ABOUT A DOZEN MANUSCRIPTS I'D be critiquing for a writers' conference. Several times I found myself underlining a phrase and simply writing "no" in the margin. Since I meet with these folks face-to-face and discuss my comments, that "no" is shorthand for "I don't think this is *exactly* what you meant to say—back up and try it again."

I think it was Mark Twain who said that writing isn't finding the right word—it's finding the exact word, for there's a vast difference between *lightning* and *lightning bug*. So many times I find that beginning writers get caught up in the story and they dash off the first metaphor, phrase, or word that comes to mind.

But writing that makes the reader stop and go "Huh?" isn't effective writing. The writer has jerked the reader out of what John Gardner calls "the vivid and continuous dream." A good writer, says Gardner, revises and revises until he gets it right, and captures it in language so "that other human beings, whenever they feel like it, may open his book and dream that dream again."

Occasionally I run across a manuscript that errs in the opposite direction—a writer who clearly cares more about words than story. Gardner says this writer "is unlikely to create a vivid and continuous dream; he gets in his own way too much—in his poetic drunkenness, he can't tell the cart—and its cargo—from the horse."

Gardner says (and this makes me smile) that such a writer should switch to poetry or find an editor and a body of readers who love fine language. "Such editors," says Gardner, "and readers do appear from time to time, refined spirits devoted to an exquisitely classy game we call fiction only by stretching the term to the breaking point."

Gardner says this kind of writer "is not likely to feel passionate attachment to the ordinary, mainstream novel. The novel's unashamed engagement with the world . . . all these are likely to seem, to the word fanatic, silly and tedious; he feels himself buried in litter."

It is at this point that I must confess my attraction to this so-called "litter." On a plane recently, I read a much-heralded book that had been much-praised by the literati. Yes, the writing was beautiful, but I found the whole thing a snooze. If I'd had anything else to read, I would have put the book away. The novelist deliberately kept the characters at arms' length, and I really didn't care about what happened to them.

Lovely words are fine, but what a reader takes from a book isn't the words—it's the *images* that sharp, exact words *create*. We may remember a cunning phrase or two, but what we internalize are the characters and the trials they face, endure, and conquer. It's Scarlett shaking her fist at the sky and promising never to be hungry again; it's the poor woman in *The Lottery* who pleads with her neighbors not to stone her; it's Tom Sawyer slyly grinning and convincing his friends to whitewash that fence.

Ah, give me a story. Give me details, sweat, grime, love, laughter, hatred, evil, fear, irritation, pearls of perspiration on a lover's upper lip. Let me live inside your villain's skin. Let me tremble with your protagonist and quake with her fury. Give me images and real life, and, if you have room, toss in a few lovely words.

As the farmer said to Babe, "That'll do, Pig."

CHAPTER THREE

I Guess I'm not a Classy Writer

DO YOU KNOW THE DIFFERENCE BETWEEN "CLASSY" AUTHORS and working writers?

Classy authors never show their toes in public. Writers go barefoot as often as they can.

Classy authors are always dressed up. Writers don't comb their hair before lunch and wear sweat suits if no one is coming over. Because I live in Florida, I'm usually in shorts with bare feet.

Classy authors never yell. Writers get excited and scream when their kids are pounding on the door, the printer won't print, or the power goes off unexpectedly. We used to live in a rural area where our power transformers were mounted atop telephone poles. I can't tell you how many times I've been hard at work, heard a large *kaboom*, and stepped outside to discover that a squirrel had committed suicide on my telephone pole. Being a dedicated *female* writer, naturally I went back into the house, called Florida Power, and went shopping.

Classy Christian authors only read newspapers, the Bible, and

My Utmost for His Highest. Working writers read those things, too. But we read the comics first thing in the morning and wistfully peek at Best Seller lists. We read other authors and gleefully note grammatical errors in the margins.

Classy authors do not eat except at banquets where they're always the speaker and guest of honor. Writers snack all the time and consequently gain two pounds per book—unless they learn to chew sugarless gum instead.

Classy authors have housekeepers who cook for their families. Writers make tons of spaghetti and memorize the phone number for any pizza place that will deliver. I'm happy to report that the Schwan man and I are now on a first name basis.

In 1983, when I started writing, I wanted to be a classy author. I'd dream about people standing in three-mile lines for my book signings or stopping me on the street and saying, "Aren't you . . .

But *five years* later, I actually wrote a book that a publisher wanted to buy. And the night after I got "the call," I lay awake thinking that the time had come to get serious, people were actually going to read what I wrote. And my words might change their lives the way some books have changed mine. And that God had just given me an awesome responsibility. . .

A couple of summers ago I went with my husband's youth group to a camp where they have horseback riding. I mounted my hot, sweaty mare and leaned forward to brush the horseflies from her face. "What's this horse's name?" I asked the trail guide.

"Classy," he said.

I grinned. I knew that was as close to classy as I would ever be.

CHAPTER FOUR

It's a Mad, Mad, Mad Crazy Lady

LAST MONTH I WAS TUCKED INTO MY HOTEL ROOM AFTER spending a delightful day in two schools--Cumberland Christian Academy in Austell and Whitefield Academy in Vinings, Georgia. I had reserved the evening for last minute polishing of *The Elevator,* which was due in less than twenty-four hours.

I had sent my manuscript to my lawyer friend Michael, who not only checked my elevator accuracy, but proved to be an excellent editor. One of his queries puzzled me: Does *te quiero* mean *I love you* or *I want you*--an important distinction if one's Mexican character is speaking to her mother.

So I left my hotel room (in my stocking feet) and padded down to housekeeping, where I could hear several women speaking in Spanish. I walked into the room and announced that I was working on a book, and asked what I thought was a polite and unassuming question: "*Habla espanol?*"

Two of the less-startled maids nodded.

I smiled. "If you want to say *I love you, mama*, es *te quiero Mama* or *te llamo Mama* o *que?*"

They gave me blank looks, but a couple of other ladies came to their aid. About that time I realized I should have asked, "*Habla Engles?*"

When the other ladies approached, I mentioned my book. One of them said, "*El libro?*"

I jumped on this sign of progress and said, "*Si, es para mi libro. Es te quiero Mama or te llamo Mama? Como dice que?*"

I, of course, had no idea if I was saying the right thing, having spoken very little Spanish since the tenth grade.

The women looked at each other, then one of them told me to go to the office.

I was halfway there—still in my stocking feet—when I realized that the folks at the Wingate front desk would have no idea how to help me.

So I hurried to my room, grabbed my laptop, and then ran into two of the housekeepers in the hallway. I pointed to the computer. "*Este es mi libro. Isabel dice que Adios, Mama. Te quiero, mama, vaya con Dios.*"

I looked at the bewildered women, hoping that words on the screen would be more effective that my babble. "*Es bueno?*"

Fortunately, they looked at the computer, then nodded. And after returning to my room, I realized I had been confusing "te amo" (I love you) with "te llamo" (I name you).

Still later, at dinner, I realized what those poor women must have seen: a mad redhead in socks running around saying, *Book, I want you mama, I name you Mama, I love you mama?*

I can only hope my readers appreciate the lengths to which I'm willing to go to get the details right.

CHAPTER FIVE

An Honest Byline

A FEW YEARS AGO, I WAS ONE OF SEVENTY-FIVE CHRISTIAN novelists who signed a letter saying that they had become increasingly concerned and dismayed about the practice of ghostwritten novels. This letter went out to all the major Christian publishing houses and our agents.

Though most publishers did *not* do this, we knew the practice was ongoing in the Christian publishing industry because some of us had been offered those jobs. We believed—and still believe—the situation is deceptive, a form of false advertising, and ultimately demeaning to the work God has called us to do.

Erickson's *Concise Dictionary of Christian Theology* defines honesty as "truthfulness, openness, and fairness in all of one's representations and business dealings." Scripture tells us: "False weights and unequal measures—the Lord detests double standards of every kind" (Prov. 20:10). Ghostwritten novels deceive the book buying public, and scandals arise when it occurs even in the secular marketplace. Why should it be condoned in the Christian publishing industry?

What are we talking about? A ghostwritten novel lists one person as the author when someone else has actually written the book. It's tantamount to plastering one of our names on a Picasso painting and taking full credit (and the sales price) when we don't know the first thing about painting. Even if one of us said, "Picasso, why don't you paint a one-eyed blue man?", that's not enough. Even if we supplied the paint, that's still not enough to take full credit for work we didn't do. Even if we paid Picasso for his labor, that doesn't give us the right to claim that we created the painting.

We are not talking about dual author teams where one person supplies ideas and research and another does the writing. We've seen many of these duos in recent years, and we have no complaint when the writers' name is listed with a partner's. We trust that they have come to an equitable arrangement to share the work, the reward, and the responsibility.

I've heard people say, "What does it matter whose name is on the cover? As long as the message gets out and God gets the credit."

Ah, but the credit is going to the person whose name is on the cover. And how is he/she supposed to react when he/she is praised for the work? Aren't we leading our brothers and sisters to bear false witness by participating in this sort of arrangement?

Someone else might say that ghostwriting is okay if a writer really needs the money to support his family. Isn't that like saying that stealing bread is okay if you're really hungry?

I used to ghostwrite nonfiction--I would take someone's materials and shape it into a book. But I became convicted even about that, because what would it matter to admit such an arrangement took place? Nothing. Perhaps we need to realize that our well-known pastors, teachers, and athletes *aren't* professional writers. Who would expect them to be?

Not too long ago a female celebrity appeared on one of the late night talk shows to talk about her new novel. She gushed about how hard it was to write, but how fun, and how she'd labored over the work . . .

I knew she hadn't written a word because an industry insider told me about her ghostwriter. Such blatant lying makes me queasy, especially since I know how much hard work goes into the crafting of a novel.

A novel is an art form that arises after years of work and studying the craft. Christian novelists are committed to excellence in our fiction, and we write to glorify God. For a publisher to propose that a novel be cranked out, stamped with a celebrity's name, and sold to an unsuspecting public demeans our work and dishonors our Lord Jesus Christ, who is the Truth.

So no more ghostwriting for me. I'll still write other people's stories, but my name has to be on the book somewhere. It doesn't have to be big, and it doesn't have to be on the cover, but it has to at least be on the title page. Because I want be honest with readers.

CHAPTER SIX

How Long Does it Take?

IN MY READING, I'VE OCCASIONALLY RUN ACROSS THE NOTION that a book produced in, say, three or four months could not possibly be as good as one produced over a decade. In fact, I'm currently reading a tome that took ten years to write . . . and I'm beginning to wonder if five wouldn't have done the job. (Just kidding. Sorta.)

Seriously—when I hear that it takes *years* for someone to write a novel, I tend to scratch my head because it's normal for me to produce a book in three to six months. But you have to realize that writing is my full-time job and I'm fairly obsessive about it. Once I manage to slide into my fictive world (and that takes some doing when there is laundry to be done, family at home, and email chiming every five minutes), I don't want to come up for hours.

When I hear about folks who work a full-time job and come home to spend time with the family and then settle down for an hour or two of working on the novel—well, I'm *impressed*. That takes dedication and incredible focus. And a willingness to turn off the TV.

So naturally it takes Writer A--who's writing full time, and obsessively--less time than Writer B, who is juggling his novel with the demands of a busy life *plus* another job. The time invested has little to do with the quality of the book (unless, of course, either author is asked to make revisions and he/she refuses to go through the process again.)

In one sense, it takes a lifetime to write a novel--*your* lifetime, as much life as you've lived to this point. Because your *life*--your history, emotions, questions, and beliefs--is the well you're going to draw from. It's the source of the passion that will fire your writing. Yes, fiction requires imagination, but story should be grounded in reality. And that's where it helps to have a rich, *other*-centered life.

If my math can be trusted, the first adult novel I wrote required about three months of writing time, eight years of writing experience, and thirty-two years of life experience. (Remember--I wrote articles and such for five years before I ever *dreamed* of writing a book, then I wrote picture books for a while.)

So let's not fool ourselves—it's not likely that anyone can sit down and write a publishable novel without any experience or instruction. While there are savants in every field, most of us need time to learn the nuts and bolts of craft. So read writing books, go to writer's conferences, take a class, join an *encouraging* critique group. Lean how to cut through literary pomposity and communicate in common language. Pay yourself a quarter for every word you can cut.

Once you learn the nuts and bolts, there is *art* to explore and master--the fine shading that makes a book stand out from the crowd of published pages. There are a thousand tools with which you can shape story: techniques such as interior monologue, standards of genre, styles, differing points of view, metaphor, etc.

Writing is a progressive endeavor; you improve as you write. In time you may move from exploring comfortable issues to delving into challenging concepts of man and God. Your goal shifts from being published to being wise . . . *because books change lives.*

I have a saying painted on the wall of my office: "The act of writing is the act of discovering what you believe." Every book—and every day at the desk—is an adventure in discovery.

So don't rush to publication. Don't send your book to one of those vanity presses. See your novel in progress as a joy and a lesson that may be published or may become a fond memory because it's where you learned how to write. And when you have reached the place where your work is acceptable to a publisher who will cherish and support it, you'll be one step closer to being the writer you want to be—one who will stand before the Master Storyteller and hear "Well done."

CHAPTER SEVEN

The Writer's Pride

I'VE BEEN RUMINATING.

I was reading good ol' C.S. Lewis the other day, *Mere Christianity,* the chapter on "the great sin." You guessed it—pride. Lewis points out that most human vices come from "our animal nature," but pride doesn't come through an animal nature, but from Hell itself. (Ever seen an animal compare itself to another?)

Lewis says that pride is essentially competitive. The fault doesn't lie in recognizing our abilities, it lies in comparing our abilities to others'. Pride doesn't want us to say we're good writers or whatever, it wants to make us think we're better than everyone else.

Lewis says, "If everyone became equally rich, or clever, or good-looking there would be nothing to be proud about. It is the comparison that makes you proud: the pleasure of being above the rest. Once the element of competition has gone, pride has gone."

That's why I remind myself that in God's ultimate reality, the earthly externals don't matter—what matters is if we were obedient to God's call, if we were good stewards with the talents and abilities we were given, and if we obeyed the prompting of the Spirit.

If we do that, and if we honor our brother and sister writers as we would honor ourselves, we are equally obedient in God's sight. Competition disappears, pride dies.

Pride, Lewis says, is spiritual cancer—it eats up the very possibility of love, or contentment, or even common sense. He points out that pleasure in being praised is not Pride. If someone says, "Well done," and you're pleased, that's okay. The trouble begins when you move from thinking, 'I have pleased him, all is well' to 'What a fine person I must be to have done it.'"

Lewis: "The more you delight in yourself and the less you delight in the praise, the worse you are becoming."

Another thing I found interesting: Pride's opposite is humility, but don't think the most humble person is the one who hangs his head and goes around moaning about how untalented he is. He has taken the pendulum of pride in the opposite direction and is still self-centered. Lewis says that if you meet a truly humble person, "probably all you will think about him is that he seemed a cheerful, intelligent chap who took a real interest in what you said to him."

Not like the writer who said, "Forgive me, I've talked about my writing enough. Tell me—what did *you* think of my book?"

One thing I've begun to do is to substitute the word *pleasure* for *proud*. When someone compliments me for a book—something that usually sends me into full-blown reject-the-compliment mode in an effort to rebuff pride, I now smile and say, "Thank you. Working on that book brought me a great deal of pleasure."

And isn't it infinitely better to be pleased with our work than proud of it? I only hope God is as pleased as I am.

May He help me to remember I am only *one* writer in a sea of others. May he help me to be faithful to my task, and supportive of everyone else's.

CHAPTER EIGHT

Writing Fast

IN HIS BOOK *OUTLIERS*, MALCOLM GLADWELL POSITED THAT achieving excellence in any given field requires at least 10,000 hours of practice.

If a writer writes eight hours a day, according to Mr. Gladwell's hypothesis, he could achieve excellence in 1,250 days or 3.42 years.

But that writing couldn't be simple typing-whatever-comes-to-mind. It would need to be deliberate practice, which would require knowledge of one's weaknesses and a determined effort to overcome them.

How many books could a writer produce in 3.42 years? Depends entirely upon the writer.

I walk fast. I type fast. I read fast. (I only wish I could *think* fast.)

I also write fast. I have friends who write faster than I do, and they're not slouches--they are award-winning, deep, thoughtful, relevant authors . . . who are almost embarrassed to admit how quickly they can write because some people think that a quickly-written book simply can't be any good.

They're wrong. I wrote my first picture book in twenty-minutes and it won first place in a national contest. Trust me, no one was more surprised than me.

Maybe we tightly-wired writers are all a little obsessive-compulsive because we simply can't let the book go once we sit down to work. I can only speak for myself, but I work long hours and tweak and twiddle and change and layer through four or five drafts, and I don't hand a manuscript over to my editor until it is as perfect and lovely as I can possibly make it. And after I get editorial feedback, I rewrite again. (Everybody does—or should.)

I'll confess something else—the longer I work at this, the slower I get. Which translates into more focus and more hours at the computer in a given day. I figure in a few years, I may be permanently fused to my office chair.

I'm not sure production speed is a credible criteria for evaluating a person's work. On some days you get caught up in the story and the words flow out of you. Maybe, for some fortunate folks, this happens almost every day.

And fast writers enjoy the benefits of cumulative effort and life lessons. Fiction requires preparation.

Recently I read an essay in Lawrence Block's book, *Spider, Spin Me a Web*. Mr. Block said he wrote *Eight Million Ways to Die* in two months, start to finish. From January 1982 through February—and February is a short month.

Then Block admitted that he'd done some outlining and plotting in December '81. And in the summer of '81, he had to come up with a logline so the publisher put something in the catalog. Two years before that, he'd been percolating on ideas and not really writing anything else, so maybe that time should count toward the writing of *Eight Million*. A few years before that, he'd had an idea about creating a story about a particular character who collected African art, and that character showed up in *Eight Million* . . . so maybe that research time should be counted, too.

Before that, he'd made a false start on a manuscript, writing

185 pages that fizzled out. But the germ of those pages made it into *Eight Million*. Before that, he'd met a man who encouraged him to do a book about a pimp, and that character made it into *Eight Million*. Before that, he'd created his protagonist, Matthew Scudder, who'd been around for years, constantly evolving and working . . . before that, Block had moved to New York City, which came to be a strong character in all the Matthew Scudder novels, including *Eight Million Ways to Die*.

So . . . since nothing in a novelist's life is wasted, perhaps we should say that it takes a lifetime to produce a novel. The book I produce in three or four or five months (through four or five drafts) has usually been percolating in my mind and heart for a long time.

Block sums it up this way: "There's as much of me as anything else in that book, and I couldn't have written it as I did without everything in my life that preceded it. I was born on June 24, 1938. It took me forty-three years and eight months to write *Eight Million Ways to Die*."

I've been writing novels for years, and now I'm using skills I didn't even *have* when I started. The writer's life is an apprenticeship, and the time it takes varies greatly from individual to individual. So enjoy what you read and don't worry about the time the writer took to produce it. Unless a writer chooses to tell you, *you don't know* how long it took . . . but if the story rings with Truth, you can almost bet it involved a lifetime.

CHAPTER NINE

Sentiment and Sentimentality

I USED TO BE CONFUSED BY THOSE TWO TERMS WHICH IS NOT good, because sentiment (i.e., emotion) in a novel is a Good Thing, while sentimentality is not. Then I heard the difference explained this way: sentimentality almost always goes for the "expected" thing, often to the point of cliché. A depiction of true sentiment covers new territory.

I don't watch much TV, but right now I'm an admitted *Alias* addict. Never watched it on TV before this season, but I rented the DVDs and I am enthralled by the writing. Never a dull moment, never a plot thread wrapped up without another one being strung out. Sydney Bristow, the protagonist, has more conflicts in her personal and professional lives than any human could realistically endure, yet she carries on with style and a smile.

Anyway, in season two (I think) Vaughn and Sydney are attracted to each other. You *know* Vaughn wants to declare his feelings, but is he going to do it in a sentimental way? Of course not.

They're together in their clandestine meeting place (spies can never meet in public, you know) and he points to his watch. "You see this watch?" he says. "My dad gave it to me. He said you could set your heart by this watch."

Sydney looks at him, waiting.

Vaughn continues: "The thing is, this watch stopped on October first. That's the day we met."

Their respective beepers go off, reminding them that Duty comes before love. Then, with tears in her eyes, Sydney looks at him and smiles and says, "Me, too."

And I want to swoon.

Why is this great dialogue? Because 1) It's unexpected. 2) It's not "on the nose." It's not tit for tat. Sydney responds to what Vaughn is thinking, (*I think I love you*), not what he's saying.

Best of all, the watch keeps showing up, and every time it does, it's laden with emotional meaning. The writers don't have to say anything, because we devoted viewers know what it means to Vaughn and what it represents between him and Sydney.

I saw another great exchange today. Sydney and Vaughn are sitting on a bench eating ice cream cones, and Syd confesses that she lied to Vaughn about a co-worker. She says she pretty much grew up alone, so she's not used to being accountable to someone, and she's sorry she lied.

Vaughn cocks a brow and we're not sure if he's going to be angry or forgiving or hurt or irritated . . . and he offers Syd a bite of his ice cream, then he stands and extends his hand.

Invisible dialogue, pure sentiment, not gushy sentimentality.

Most of us have a little writer inside us who is constantly predicting what a character will say--and in a lot of movies and TV shows, I find myself able to parrot dialogue along with the characters because the setup and following lines are so predictable. I've never been able to do that with *Alias*. And that's a delight.

I'm a fan. As if you couldn't tell.

CHAPTER TEN

Ender's Game

I LIKE TO TRAVEL, BUT I *LOVE* AIRPLANE TIME BECAUSE IT'S about the only time in my life where I don't feel guilty about sitting down and reading.

For my airplane book a few weeks ago, I chose *Ender's Game* by Orson Scott Card —and was blown away. I especially loved the ending. See if it strikes you the same way it strikes me. (SPOILER ALERT—if you want to read the book, don't read further.)

Backstory: Ender Wiggin, a child, has been trained since the age of six to fight in space. By the age of twelve, he is playing "video games" in space, only to discover that he has actually killed the queen of the "buggers," an ant-like race who came to invade the earth twice before. Humankind has enlisted Ender because they want to launch a third strike and kill all the buggers before they can come again to invade Earth.

So Ender, thinking he's commanding a fleet in a video training game, completely destroys all life on the bugger planet. Years later he discovers a place on the planet that is like one of his frequent dreams, and he realizes that the collective consciousness of the bugger queen has invaded his mind and constructed this place to relay a message, which Ender relates to humankind:

> It was written as if the hive-queen spoke, telling all that they had meant to do, and all that they had done. Here are our failures, and here is our greatness; we did not mean to hurt you, and we forgive you for our death. From their earliest awareness to the great wars that swept across their home world, Ender told the story quickly, as if it were an ancient memory. When he came to the tale of the great mother, the queen of all, who first learned to keep and teach the new queen instead of killing her or driving her away, then he lingered, telling how many times she had to destroy the child of her body, the new self that was not herself, until she bore one who understood her quest for harmony. This was a new thing in the world, two queens that loved and helped each other instead of battling, and together they were stronger than any other hive. They prospered; they had more daughters who joined them in peace; it was the beginning of wisdom. (Orson Scott Card, *Ender's Game,* Tor Science Fiction, 1994).

Okay, back to my point: I know one can see truth in just about anything, but I see so *much* in the above paragraph! I see God creating men and finding only a few who will seek him; I see the church; I see a body of Christian writers who can come together instead of battling for preeminence.

Science fiction is usually not my first choice of genre for reading or writing, but I'd heard so many things about this book I thought I'd give it a read. And even though it was written more than thirty years ago and breaks a lot of today's "writing rules," it's a *great* story.

And there's this from the introduction by Orson Scott Card: "Why else do we read fiction, anyway? Not to be impressed by somebody's dazzling language—or at least I hope that's not our reason. I think that most of us, anyway, read these stories that we know are not 'true' because we're hungry for another kind of truth: the mythic truth about human nature in general, the particular truth about those life-communities that define our own identity, and the most specific truth of all: our own self-story. Fiction, because it is not about somebody who actually lived in the real world, always has the possibility of being about ourselves."

And that profound thought is worth pondering all day.

CHAPTER ELEVEN

Broadcasting Foolishness

I WAS READING THE OTHER NIGHT AND RAN HEADLONG INTO this quote by Jane Smiley in *13 Ways of Looking At the Novel*: "If to live is to progress, if you are lucky, from foolishness to wisdom, then to write novels is to broadcast the various stages of your foolishness."

I think that's one of the most profound statements I've read lately. The other day I was talking to a friend about how my theology had changed since I really began to study theology . . . and how I once wrote a novel predicated on the idea that God has a permissive will and a perfect will, and that we can fall short of the latter and have to settle for the former.

"But I don't believe that any more," I said. "I believe that in God's sovereignty, everything I do, even my mistakes, are part of his plan. Why do we always assume that mistakes are bad? That tragedy is undesirable? Because God is going to use even these things to mold us into the people He wants us to be."

Those of us who've been writing for a long time often cringe when we think about our early books because our writing styles have changed—most of us tend to write tighter and leaner with experience. (I edited a book for re-publication the other day and cut out 9,000 completely unnecessary words).

But there are other things that change as well. Novels, like it or not, *do* put forth a worldview; characters learn lessons and change in ways that reflect the author's view of life. So it's crucial that we *get it right* from an eternal perspective.

The responsibility could be overwhelming, if you thought about it very long or very deeply. Those of us who are believers are presenting and/or justifying the ways of God to man . . . as if He needed our help . . . and yet He chooses to use us.

Wow.

Jane Smiley says that a novel is an *ontological construct*, which is a fifty-cent way of saying that a novel says, "the world is like *this*." Smiley also says "as every novelist has a style, so every novelist has conviction" . . . and convictions can change. Which is a good thing, because, according to Smiley , "if the conviction simply dissipates or grows stale, the novels do, too."

So I'm glad I'm changing some of my convictions and adopting new perspectives. As I grow as a person and as a follower of Christ, my work will grow, too. But if I'm saying "God is like this . . .", I must take pains to speak the truth.

So . . . what have I done about the novel based on a premise I no longer support? I went back and skimmed it . . . and found that the premise is so subtle, I doubt many people will pick it up. And I've written a new book, *The Novelist*, about the sovereignty of God and how it works in our lives.

But the experience has reminded me of my responsibility as a novelist: to take every care to get it right.

CHAPTER TWELVE

Voice

RECENTLY I WAS READING A THREAD ON A WRITER'S GROUP about voice. I'd also just returned from a writer's workshop where voice came up, and as I looked around the room at my fellow students, I had the feeling that some folks were confused.

But "voice" need not be confusing. When we talk about a writer's voice, are we referring to the voice of his characters? Yes. Of his narrator? Yes. The voice inherent in his exposition? Yes.

In short, a writer's "voice" is found in every word in the book. A writer's voice is unique whether he or she is writing a romance, a young adult novel, even a nonfiction book. Why? Because when a writer is confident and operating on his or her best instincts, writer's voice is wholly his or her own.

The writer's voice springs from some place deep inside. If you are true to yourself and don't try to imitate some other writer, you will find your authentic voice.

I remember one day many years ago when I was reviewing one of my manuscripts that had just come through the substantive edit. I never compare the final edit with my submission draft unless something doesn't seem right—and suddenly I nearly spurted my Diet Coke across the page. I read a line—I don't remember exactly what it was, but it talked about someone being a goon or a hunk or something—and I knew that I wouldn't use the phrase on the page in a hundred years of writing. Not that there was anything wrong with the words, they just weren't "me."

Sure enough, the editor had done a bit of rewriting, and when I pointed it out, she was quick to tell me to take out her edit and rephrase it myself. So I did.

I was reading Jane Smiley's *13 Ways of Looking at the Novel* earlier this year and I liked what she said about voice, though she referred to it as *diction*:

> Even in a sentence or two, the reader apprehends not only what the author is thinking of, but also how he or she thinks—with hesitations and qualifications, sharply and straightforwardly, conversationally, contemplatively. Each author's diction is characteristic, and so is his or her sense of rhythm and directness. His or her mental life, at least with regard to that particular subject, is more and more perfectly expressed by the style he or she uses. He is artful; he chooses; he manipulates; he decides; he judges every word and sound pattern and character detail and twist in the action, and yet every one of these things is automatic, given, natural, right. The mind writing is no longer made of parts—the conscious and the subconscious, the voluntary and the involuntary; it is rather one integrated whole, focused and choosing, from all the words in the language, the single perfect one. And the closer the author comes to his or her true stylistic self, the more distinct he becomes from every other writer who has ever written and the more precious he becomes to the reader. (Jane Smiley, *13 Ways of Looking at the Novel*, Anchor Books, 2006).

Your writing voice may be hard for you to define because it is everything about you—the words you choose, the metaphors you employ, the rhythm, the cadence, the resonance . . . As Jane said, the more you relax and let yourself be yourself, the stronger your voice will become.

So write on and don't worry about your voice—as long as you are true to yourself (i.e., don't try to imitate someone else), your voice will be there.

CHAPTER THIRTEEN

Life-Fillers and Life-Drainers

A LOT OF PEOPLE SPEND ALL THEIR TIME BLOGGING ABOUT things they *could* write--if they didn't spend all their time blogging.

Aw, don't think I'm picking on you. The above saying applies to me as much as anyone because I haven't even *begun* my daily quota and the clock is ticking. But when you feel a Spirit nudge, you gotta go with it . . .

The point is this: if you are going to become accomplished at any professional activity, you're going to have to spend hours involved in that professional activity. For the writer, this means hours with your rear in a chair while you read or write over and over again. For the Christian writer, it means viewing your daily activities in the light of eternal perspectives.

It also means you have to put up some guards around your twenty-four hours in a day. But this isn't a post on time management. Because in order to have something to write about, you have to have a life, and in order to have a life, you have to haul yourself out of that chair now and then.

I've discovered in my forty-plus years that life is filled with activities that can suck you in like the Mafia. The evil one would love to distract us from doing what is *best* with doing what is harmful, neutral, or merely *good*. The trick is learning to discern which activities are life-fillers and which are life-drainers. What may be an "LF" for me may be an "LD" for you, and vice versa. But here are some specific examples from my experience.

Life-drainer: accepting a position on my neighborhood's board of directors.

Life-filler: starting a neighborhood book club (where we frequently discuss spiritual themes).

Life-drainer: working seven days a week.

Life-filler: taking a Sabbath and keeping it holy.

Life-drainer: bad books, bad movies, bad TV.

Life-filler: good books, good movies, great TV.

Life-drainer: trying to exercise someone else's spiritual gift.

Life-filler: exercising mine.

Life-drainer: joining a fitness club.

Life-filler: hitting the treadmill every morning while watching good TV.

Life-drainer: trying to be all things to all people.

Life-filler: finding my God-ordained niche and filling it.

. . .

Miscellaneous life-drainers: purposeless meetings, trying to maintain fake nails, window shopping, foolish arguments, email chain letters and urban myths.

Miscellaneous life-fillers: any time spent encouraging children, a good hair cut, time spent with my hubby, shopping with a purpose, riveting debates with friends who speak the truth in love, going back to school to keep learning.

In order to fill your creative well, you have to let LIFE drop into it. In order to maintain your spiritual life, you have to feed it daily. God has placed you in a specific place, time, and situation for a reason . . . and you need to examine the elements of your life and make sure you're using your time in the best way possible.

"For what is your life?" James asked. "It is only a vapor that appears for a little time and then vanishes away."

Your life is time. You have a finite amount in your account. Spend it wisely in the light of God's eternal purposes.

CHAPTER FOURTEEN

Invictus!

BETCHA DIDN'T KNOW THAT I TOOK FENCING IN COLLEGE. YEP.
I wasn't very skilled, but I won a couple of matches because my
opponents didn't expect a (mostly) ladylike gal to attack like a
caffeine-laced woman with PMS.

A few months ago I was working on a book set in ancient
Rome/Palestine. In my research about the Roman army, I ran
across this quote:

"The drill for weapon training was introduced to the soldiers by
the consul P. Rutilius . . . for he did not follow the precedent of
any commander before him, but instead he summoned the
trainers of gladiators from the school of Aurelius Scaurus and
created in the legions a more sophisticated system of avoiding and
delivering blows. *He united courage with craft and craft with courage:
craft was made bolder by the vehemence of courage, courage more circum-*

spect by the awareness of craft." (G.R. Watson, *The Roman Soldier,* Cornell University Press, 1985).

Ah ha! I had a personal epiphany when I read that statement. I saw an immediate parallel to writing Christian fiction. Instead of doing what has always been done, try looking outside the current market for a "more sophisticated system" of writing. But don't jump in unprepared--study up first. Unite the vehemence of courage with the awareness of craft!

Now-- I'm *not* saying we should copy the world's literature by creating stories that contain more sex, more violence, more profanity. That'd be taking the easy way out. That'd be like a soldier trying to imitate a dishonorable gladiator who goes for the Roman equivalent of a sucker punch . That kind of fighting resulted in a collective thumbs-down, and you *know* what that meant.

"More like what's already out there" is not better. Better is more *skillful.* Better is a more thoughtful attack.

I'm suggesting that we look to literature that is **widely read** and works to uphold the higher ideals--which are *holy* ideals first and foremost--and try to discover what makes those books work. And then let us be courageous enough to write unique stories, tempering our ideas with the circumspection of careful craft. Quality *is* important.

When I started writing novels, I went to my publisher and said, "What's selling now? What would you like me to write?" Many books later an editor said to me, "What do *you* want to write?" and suddenly the heavens rolled back. What did I want to write? The possibilities were endless . . .

That was the day I began to discover the writer God had called me to be--the earlier days were my training camp. In the early books I learned how to run and leap, to parry and thrust. I learned the rules of engagement. In the later books, I've had to call on reserves of courage to tackle difficult and even risky issues and fortify my courage with craft in order to pull it off. Now I see that I've been learning to write like a gladiator.

Now you'll have to excuse me—I'm off to flail away at a couple of uncooperative chapters.

Invictus!

CHAPTER FIFTEEN

Excuse Me While I Tread Water

"SO . . . ARE YOU JUST *SWIMMING* IN MONEY?"

The question came from an elementary-age boy while I held a Q&A session for students in the gym. As always, the teachers gasped at his chutzpah, but I smiled. I get that question all the time.

To answer him, I held up one of my big, shiny picture books. "Do you see this book?" I asked. "In the store, it sells for about $15.00. Of that $15.00, how much do you think the author gets?"

Immediately the kids began to shout out answers. "Fourteen dollars!"

"High."

"Thirteen dollars!"

"Still high."

"Seventeen dollars!" While the math teachers looked chagrinned, I repeated the question: "Of the *fifteen* dollars, how much do you think goes to the author?"

"Ten dollars?"

"Still high."

And so we counted down to the correct answer, which some bright child eventually called out: "Fifty cents?"

"Yes, that's right. About fifty cents."

And suddenly all those bright faces that had been convinced they were in the presence of wealthy celebrity dulled to the pallor of pity. The Visiting Author wasn't swimming in money—apparently she wasn't even getting her toes wet.

Which brings me to my topic—a subject everyone wants to talk about but no one wants to mention. How much money is involved in the writing of books?

The answer is simple: Sell many books, earn many monies. Sell a few books, earn a few dollars. Sell a few books consistently, and you'd better look for a day job to support your writing habit.

The other day I found this interesting snippet in *Publishers Weekly*:

Here's the reality of the book industry: in **2004**, 950,000 titles out of the 1.2 million tracked by Nielsen Bookscan sold fewer than 99 copies. Another 200,000 sold fewer than 1,000 copies. Only 25,000 sold more than 5,000 copies. The average book in America sells about 500 copies. Those blockbusters are a minute anomaly: only 10 books sold more than a million copies last year, and fewer than 500 sold more than 100,000.

Of course, I suspect that the 1.2 million tracked books includes anything with an ISBN, including self-published books, but this is still an amazing statistic. If you do the math, you'll see that lots of folks are writing purely for the love of it.

A friend and I once co-wrote a series about a delightful little town. There are five still-in-print books in the series, and not a week goes by that we don't get letters begging us to write more. But when I ask where these folks are getting their books, the answer is usually "the library, from a friend, or on ebay/half.com."

I can certainly appreciate living on a tight budget, but unless someone *buys* the book, we can't write any more. Publishers have to make a profit to stay in business; writers have to earn a living. (Even Christian publishers and Christian writers.) So while I'm grateful for libraries and I *love* eBay, they don't do much to keep a book in print once the initial print run has been sold. In addition, any book that's co-written means that the advance money is split between two people, so they are earning half as much as they usually earn on a project.

I'll be honest—I've written over 100 books, and though my novels go out of print about as steadily as they come *into* print, I've got quite a few volumes out there earning fifty cent pieces. I make a decent living, enough that I'm able to write full time. But a couple of years ago, due to circumstances too complicated to discuss here, we found ourselves living off our home equity line. Even a prolific writer's life can be feast or famine.

Many writers have a spouse who helps support the family in the learning years and during those long lulls between checks. Sometimes the writer is the primary breadwinner. Many novelists work a day job and write at night. (More than you might think.)

And even once you become established, there are other things to consider. In the past couple of years I've made some decisions that resulted in a huge difference in our family finances.

First, I stopped ghostwriting. Ghosting can be lucrative, especially if you write books that eventually become best sellers, but after a while I couldn't help but notice that the practice of ghosting did little to serve the interest of writers. At first I justified it by saying, "They're hiring me for my expertise," but after a while I became convinced that the laborer is not only worthy of his hire, he's worthy of his byline. What does it hurt anyone to admit they had help to write a book? It costs a little pride, that's all. And giving the writer his/her due uplifts the work that all writers do. Otherwise, it feels the writer is prostituting his talent.

So I stopped ghosting and our income fell by more than half. Second, I stopped taking on other nonfiction sideline projects, too, because I began to feel that the Lord was calling me to write some specific stories—and specific *types* of stories. To be truthful,

I earn less writing my books than writing someone else's, but that's okay. I'm responsible for following God's call on my life . . . as are you.

A lot of people don't understand all that goes into the writing of a novel. For instance, the other day I gave a talk in a local library. A man stood up and told me he had a great idea, but he wanted to find a writer to write it for him. I shook my head. "Novelists have their own ideas," I said, "and, frankly, ideas are a dime a dozen. If you want to be a novelist, then do the work. Learn the craft. Learn how to shape the idea into a story. Don't hire someone to do it for you."

I've been in this business a long time and as the years have slipped by, I've changed my ideas about lots of things. But I've never regretted my decision to stop ghosting. Nor have I rued my decision to concentrate on the stories the Lord gives me, no matter how many copies sell. God has always proven himself faithful.

The result? A life of living by faith for finances, ideas, and opportunities. A lot of belt-tightening. A lot of risk-taking.

So excuse me while I go tread water.

2013 update: the publishing industry is even more finically strained now than it was when I first wrote this piece. Publishers are struggling, and mergers are occurring all over the place, so there are now fewer places to sell a writer's work. Traditional publishers are also more risk-adverse, so they're offering lower advances and fewer contracts.

Self-publishing is always an option, of course, but the market has been flooded with self-published books, many of which could have benefitted from a serious edit and a few more years in the writer's imagination. How do you make your book stand out in the midst of that flood? We're all still trying to figure it out.

Just know this: the average working writer isn't rich. Stephen King has done well, and John Grisham, and others whose names you regularly see on the best-seller lists. But most of us are working for what would probably measure out to minimum wage if you divided the advance (minus expenses and commissions) by the number of hours we invest into a book.

Really.

CHAPTER SIXTEEN

Called to Obey

I OFTEN HEAR CHRISTIANS SAY THEY HAVE BEEN CALLED TO DO this or that—called to be a writer, a teacher, a pastor, etc. And Scripture does say that some of us have been called to be pastors, teachers, administrators, and the like, but that passage is talking about how we have been gifted . . . and how we're expected to use those gifts in the Body and for the kingdom.

When I was writing *The Debt*, I did a search of Scripture—was there anything else to which we are definitely called? And I found one main thing from which everything else stems—we are called to love and obey God. Period. That's it. God doesn't speak of calling anyone else to do anything else but obey. In the Scripture, He is constantly calling people to obey.

I'm serving God as a writer now, but I'm also serving him as a mother, a wife, a sometime columnist, a neighbor, a photographer, and a woman on the street. In the past I've served him as a singer, a student, a secretary, a teacher, and a cashier. Wherever you are in life, you are to love and obey God where you are. That's your calling.

My calling—and yours—may change tomorrow. The woman who's obeying God as a teacher today may obey him as a missionary tomorrow. The things we often think of as permanent "callings" are anything but permanent . . . *if* we remain open to the will of God and are willing to obey him. He does not always lead down well-paved interstates. Sometimes he leads over twisty, circuitous paths. But always, he is leading.

Most people ask me if I've always wanted to be a writer. They expect to hear that I grew up writing, or that I was scribbling stories as a child. Well . . . no. I have always loved reading and I did try my hand at a short story when I was in about fifth grade. But I never felt especially good at writing, nor did I ever think I'd be doing anything with it.

One thing I did know—I had accepted Jesus Christ as my savior when I was six years old, so I knew my life belonged to him. I didn't know how he would use it or where he would take me, but I knew I was His and that He had a plan for me. I also knew that God would tell me what he wanted me to do in three ways: through His Word, the Bible; through the leading of my parents and spiritual leaders, and through His voice.

My job is simply to obey.

When God was about to create man, says a Jewish legend, He took into His counsel the angels that stood about his throne. "Create him not," said the angel of Justice, "for if you do he will commit all kinds of wickedness against his fellow men; he will be hard and cruel and dishonest and unrighteous."

"Create him not," said the angel of Truth, "for he will be false and deceitful to his brother-man, and even to You."

"Create him not," said the angel of Holiness, "he will follow that which is impure in your sight, and blaspheme you to your face."

Then stepped forward the angel of Mercy and said: "Create him, our Heavenly Father, for when he sins and turns from the path of right and truth and holiness I will take him tenderly by the hand, and speak loving words to him, and then lead him back to You."

Whether you are a speaker, a writer, a mom, a teacher, a father, or a carpenter, or a cashier, we are called to show God's mercy to the world because first and foremost, we are called to love and obey God. Just like the angels.

I pray we never forget that.

CHAPTER SEVENTEEN

Open your Eyes to Opportunity

I TEACH AT A LOT OF WRITERS' CONFERENCES—I THINK THIS year I'll do seven-- and I've noticed that almost everybody either actively or secretly wants to write a novel. That's great, I happen to love fiction and think it's the hardest form to master. I'm still learning the craft of novel writing, and it's still a challenge.

But I feel I'd be remiss if I didn't toss out another challenge to all the would-be novelists in the world. Don't work *only* on your novel. When you feel that nudge of the Spirit, when a topic rouses your passion, start writing *now*, and let your words make a difference.

I wrote brochures, catalog copy, and articles before I even thought about writing a book. I wrote half a dozen picture books before I even considered writing novels for children. I wrote about thirty novels for children before an editor ever suggested, "You know, why don't you try writing for adults?"

My point: I was learning while I wrote, plus I was earning a living. The financial income was important, but more important than the income or the learning was this: My words were making a difference while I was learning. I pray that's still true.

I am delighted that God is calling so many of his children to exercise their pens. There is power in the printed word, and the words have the power to change lives. Look at all the books that have altered the course of American history: *A Silent Spring* by Rachel Carson and *Uncle Tom's Cabin* by Harriet Beecher Stowe, just to name two.

But don't linger behind the curtain while you dream of publishing a book. Don't spend so much time "suffering for your art" that you're of no practical use to the Kingdom of God.

If God has given you a "way with words," exercise that gift every day. Don't hide your views under the proverbial bushel. Our society needs to hear from people with Christian values and well-reasoned convictions. Your neighbors need to hear Truth proclaimed from the housetops and the editorial pages. Your denominational magazines need articles that put a proper spine in jelly theology. We live in a dark world, and people are hungry for light.

My local newspaper, *The Tampa Tribune*, held an "audition" one year for "community columnists." These people would be allowed to write columns on the editorial page about any topic whatsoever, as long as it wasn't blatantly self-promotional. I sent in a writing sample, and when my hubby called to tell me I'd been selected, I was as thrilled as I've ever been about a book contract. Over the year I was a columnist, I was able to write about pro-life issues, man being created in the image of God, and racism. I had an open mike to discuss things that matter. I was edited, but not censored.

So while you're working on that novel or short story, keep your eyes and ears open for opportunities to express yourself. *Any* writing for publication will hone your skills. Be a willing tool that God can use anywhere, and remember that obedience today is far more important than pursuing your dreams of tomorrow. God wants servants he can use when he taps them on the shoulder . . . and directs them to pick up a pen.

CHAPTER EIGHTEEN

Responding to Critics

MY HUSBAND CAME TO THE BREAKFAST TABLE WITH A BOOK IN hand. While I munched on my Lucky Charms, he read me the devotional he'd found in Lloyd John Ogilvie's *God's Best for My* Life (the entry for March 7th). When he'd finished reading, I was wishing I could be more like Michelangelo.

The story is told that when Michelangelo had completed his sculpture of David, the governor of Florence came to look at the finished work. He was pleased with what he observed, but as he looked at it he dared to offer a criticism. "The nose . . . the nose is too large, is it not?"

Michelangelo looked carefully at David and quietly answered, "Yes, I think it is a little too large." He picked up a chisel and a mallet, and also a handful of marble dust, and mounted the scaffolding. Carefully he hammered, permitting small amounts of dust to fall to the ground with each blow. He finally stopped and asked, "Now look at the nose. It is correct?"

"Ah," responded the governor, "I like it . . . I like it much better. You have given it life."

Michelangelo descended, according to the old chronicle, "with great compassion for those who desire to appear to be good judges of matters whereof they know nothing."

What maturity the great artist displayed in being able to take criticism! But we wonder about the right of that governor to criticize in an area where he was not an expert.

When I receive critical letters—and trust me, I've gotten letters and emails about my choice of topic, language, and characters—I try to put my natural defensiveness aside and see if the writer hasn't discerned something I was too blind to see. If they have made a good point, I write them back and thank them for taking the time and finding the courage to write.

If, however, there is no nugget of truth, I may very well write back with blunt honesty. One Christian woman wrote and reported that she not only didn't like my book, but she was going to tell her church librarian to pull all my books from the shelves.

I wrote her back and asked one simple question: "You didn't pray about sending that email before you sent it, did you?"

She wrote back and apologized for being out of line.

Many of my friends ignore critical letters altogether, and that's certainly a valid approach because you can't reason with angry people—when people are angry, their brains cease to function rationally and they respond only with emotion.

But the Bible tells me to answer someone who has something against me. They may not expect an answer to their note (in fact, I think some critics don't believe authors read their emails), but I'm happy to reply. And as long as I do it without anger, I can usually provide a rational response.

But oh, how I wish I could respond as cleverly as Michelangelo.

CHAPTER NINETEEN

What is Good Writing?

SOMEONE ONCE ASKED ME, "WHAT IS GOOD WRITING?"

If you asked six different people that question, you'd get six different opinionated answers, so I'll add my notions to the mix.

First, I have to refer to my high school English teacher, who insisted upon giving us two grades for every writing assignment: one for technique, one for content. (I did the same thing when I taught English.) Content equals the story, which includes the element of emotional contact. Technique, on the other hand, pertains to how well the writer exercises his craft to create meaningful content. Too many technique errors draw the reader's attention away from the content and diminish the enjoyment of the story. Too little story . . . well, I won't read the book long enough to notice good technique.

The value of content can be subjective. A novel that is too in love with the sound of its own voice will leave me cold. I prefer stories that follow the mythical pattern—an interesting, active protagonist strives to reach a goal, overcomes complications, learns a lesson, sacrifices something in the effort, and comes out either a winner or a loser, but always wiser for the effort and changed by the struggle. If I can identify with the protagonist, so much the better. If his world is fascinating, even better. If I, the reader, learn something, better yet. If the novel makes me think and question my previously held suppositions, wonderful. And if a writer can do all of the above in his/her story, that's *excellent* story-telling.

What's good technique? Crisp, clear, precise writing. Using the exactly right word, and not a syllable more or less. Oblique dialogue. Clear interior dialogue uncluttered by "she thought," "he wondered," and italics. Strong verbs and nouns that obviate the need for redundant adjectives and adverbs. Exposition that flows naturally when I need it, not a moment before or after, and definitely not in dialogue between people who would already know the information.

I am peeved by the following words if they catch my attention: *that, was, were, it, suddenly*. I also like clear point of view, limited to one person per scene, because I'm a child of the video age and accustomed to thinking like a camera.

Yet when all is said and done, the most beautiful prose in the world won't matter one whit if I don't care a *lot* about the characters by the second chapter . . . some would say the second page. A gripping story will make me forgive--even not notice--all kinds of technique problems. But when I pick up a book and flip through the pages, it's the technique problems that catch my eye.

Point one: good writing captivates the reader with story and sympathetic characters.

Point two: good writing technique functions like a smooth highway. It paves the way so the story can flow without distracting the reader.

. . .

Point three: for the Christian novelist who wants to make a real difference in the world, art must serve the message, not vice versa.

(And don't tell me that novels shouldn't have messages—all novels have messages that reflect the author's world view.)

While I'm all for beautiful writing, I'd place ministry above art on my priority list. I believe that the novelist who is a Christian has a responsibility to think of his reader first and foremost. They have picked up my book because they want to be either entertained, enlightened, moved, challenged, or inspired. If I can't meet their need, I'm not doing an effective job. Not every reader is going to love every book, of course, but it's my job to know my typical reader and try to fulfill her desires.

Being a novelist isn't about satisfying the author's needs and whims. It's about others. A dentist works with craft and skill to care for his patients' teeth. A plumber works to solve his customers' plumbing problems. A teacher strives to impart wisdom. A writer writes to please her target reader.

A novelist writes a story that says "life is like this." And in that effort, he or she illustrates the truth about sin and sacrifice, grace and justice, love and loss.

A novel written with passion, skill, and the reader in mind is an example of good writing.

CHAPTER TWENTY

Procrastination made Perfect

A FEW DAYS AGO I READ AN ASSOCIATED PRESS ARTICLE ABOUT the dangers of procrastination—dangers with which I, a self-employed writer, am well-acquainted. In order to pace myself and meet an impending deadline, I give myself a daily assignment . . . and then I fritter the morning away with email and Spider Solitaire. When it becomes apparent that I'll be up late unless I get to work, I open my word processing file and begin to write.

University of Calgary professor Piers Steel, a Canadian industrial psychologist, recently completed a study on procrastination and its effects. The ten-year study—which, interestingly enough, was supposed to be completed in five years—discovered that procrastination makes people poorer, fatter, and unhappier.

Professor Steel's thirty-page report, published by the American Psychological Association, found that only 5 percent of the American public thought of themselves as procrastinators in 1978 while today the figure is closer to 26 percent. Why the surge in dedicated delayers? For one thing, we have more distractions than we did in '78: instead of working, Americans can watch TiVo, surf the Internet, talk on our cell phones, play video games, listen to our iPods, and email friends with our Blackberries.

Steel estimates that the U.S. gross national product might rise by fifty billion dollars if our computers lost the "You've got mail" .wav file and the envelope icon that appears at the bottom of our screens when new email arrives. I didn't intend to test Mr. Steel's theory, but during a major computer malfunction last week, I lost my .wav file and the new mail icon. The result? I'm neither thinner, richer, nor happier. In fact, I'm probably wasting more time than usual because I keep checking my inbox.

How does procrastination make us poorer? According to Professor Steel, a delay in filing taxes on average costs an individual $400 a year. Since that seems like an unusually high figure for interest on a delayed refund, I can only assume he's referring to those who file past the deadline and have to pay penalties along with their taxes.

I can easily understand why procrastination results in weight gain. I've lost count of the oversized "last suppers" I've enjoyed before the diet which always begins tomorrow. Diets were designed for New Year's Days and Mondays. Ditto for exercise plans.

Does procrastination make us unhappier? Only if we're forced to pay $400 in back taxes and penalties, I suspect. Or late fees on the loan payment or credit card. But for every man who suffers regret because he waited too long to snag an opportunity, I'm sure there is another who is glad he took time to look—and play a game of computer Solitaire—before he leapt.

A wise person knows better than to procrastinate in certain situations—if you are sick, you should go to the doctor. If you spot a leak, call a plumber. If you notice raging flames, dial 911. Delay will only compound obvious problems.

Yet procrastination has undeniable benefits. Creativity often needs time to flex its muscles, so if you hit a wall while working on a perplexing problem, stop. Take a walk, play a game of Minesweeper, file a fingernail. The more mindless the alternate activity, the more brain cells available to your subconscious.

Procrastination can be an ally when dealing with emotional situations. Problems that looked insurmountable at six p.m. often resume manageable proportions after a good night's sleep. Raging tempers can cool when left unattended. Even grief eases when life settles back into its daily rhythm, which is probably why people who have lost a spouse are encouraged to wait a year before making drastic life changes.

Even the intellect can be aided by procrastination. The gems of knowledge are often unappreciated until we are able to put them in the proper setting. I couldn't enjoy the study of history as a high school student; now I am fascinated by people of the past. Why do college professors routinely praise continuing education students? Because adult students drink deeply at the fountain of knowledge while their younger counterparts (often) gargle.

In his *Confessions*, St. Augustine admitted that even his prayers were laced with procrastination: "*Da mihi castitatem et continetiam, sed noli modo,*" he prayed, or, in words that would probably make Professor Steel shudder, "give me chastity and continence, but not yet."

CHAPTER TWENTY-ONE

In Mr. Rogers' Neighborhood

LAST WEEK MY FRIEND ANNIE JONES TOLD ME A STORY ABOUT Fred Rogers. Seems when he was in seminary and learning all about public speaking, Fred attended a small church and heard another man preach. The minister didn't follow the "how to preach" rules and the subject matter didn't inspire Fred. He sat in his pew and mentally tore the message apart . . . and then he noticed that the woman beside him was totally enthralled. "That's just what I needed to hear today," she whispered to Fred Rogers.

And Fred said that's when he realized the "space" between a minister (or writer or singer) and a listener (or reader) is sacred. From that day forward he promised to not insert himself into someone else's sacred space. He could celebrate the fact that someone, somewhere needed to hear that message.

Being a music major in college nearly ruined me for most church music. I couldn't listen to another singer or choir without noticing (and quietly cringing) every time I heard a note that was sharp or flat or a vibrato that went *way* out of control. The little I had learned--and this is when intellect can become a dangerous thing--fostered a critical spirit within me.

And then I realized that all the joy of church music had vanished for me. To restore it, I had to learn to zip the lip of my inner critic . . . just as Fred Rogers did. I didn't know about the concept of "sacred space" back then, but I wish I had.

Ah, how faithful the Lord is to remind his children of their proper place. If we don't humble ourselves, He will do what it takes to remind us that we are servants . . . for it's in service that true joy lies. And it's in the "sacred space" between author and reader, preacher and hearer, singer and listener, that the Spirit works.

CHAPTER TWENTY-TWO

Watch the Hand

I've spent the last twenty-four hours agonizing over whether to use "slacks" or "dress pants" in a sentence, so my dogs have been a welcome distraction. While I was playing with them, I had a profound epiphany explained best in simple words.

I live with two 200 pound mastiffs. Charley Gansky, the four-year-old, is a big wimp, but he's smart. Babe, our three-year-old rescued mastiff, is territorial and as thick as a brick.

You throw a bone to Charley, he catches it. You throw a bone to Babe—she goes cross-eyed as it hits her on the nose.

Babe—who likes to throw herself at our glass front door whenever a stranger approaches--has broken so much glass that I've taken to setting one of the dining room chairs in front of the door. Semi-permanently. She doesn't realize she could move the chair with one swipe of her massive paw.

Charley, on the other hand, lets nothing stand in his way. When he wants something, he moves chairs, pushes fences, and opens latched doors. Fortunately, he's not into throwing himself at glass partitions.

How did I determine their IQs? There's one simple test. When I point to something in the other room, Charley looks in the other room. When I point out something to Babe, she looks at my hand.

Silly dog.

To train a dog to look where you're pointing, *you have to make the object being pointed out more interesting than your hand.*

And this is where the lesson applies to fiction. If I focus on pretty words, flowing language, or musical metaphors, the reader will look at my hand. It's not that my reader is as dense as Babe, it's that I, the author, am intruding. Maybe even showing off.

The trick is to make the object in the distance (ultimately the message of the story) more interesting than my language. If I can pull it off, I'll have a happy reader.

Now . . . *slacks* or *dress pants*. Which draws attention to my hand?

CHAPTER TWENTY-THREE

Fingernails

YOU CAN JUDGE SOME WRITERS' DEVELOPMENT OF THE WORK-in-progress by examining his/her fingernails.

I don't know what it is about fingernails that captivates most writers. I can be typing along, completely immersed in the story, and suddenly I stop to stare at--you guessed it, a fingernail. For some reason, that tiny sliver of white atop each finger possesses an extraordinary fascination. I study its curve, its condition, I feel for any rough spots--which must promptly be smoothed out with a file, emery board, the edge of the scotch tape dispenser, whatever I have on hand.

Please understand--I am not a particularly high maintenance woman. When the writing is going well, the fingernail fascination eases. But when words are coming like a breech baby, it's all I can do to stop staring at my hands. I'd sit on them, but then *no* words would make it to the screen.

Since I am officially going public with this rarely-acknowledged bit of writer trivia, I thought I'd fill you in on a few nail details: thumb nails grow faster than the rest of the fingernails. Big toe nails grow faster then other toenails. Toe nails grow more slowly than fingernails. Nails do not continue to grow after death (contrary to all the rumors I heard in high school).

Years ago, before I even thought about writing as a career, I read an Erma Bombeck column in which she acknowledged that a hangnail could stop her creativity cold. Now I understand.

Did I mention that fingernails often play a role in various means of torture? Evil masterminds can insert sharp objects under the nails, remove the nails with pliers, chip a coat of nail polish--any of the above would render me useless for work.

Last week I had a perfect set of lovely half-moons, one above each finger. This week I have five perfect nails and five barely-there slivers--the result of overzealous filing because the words aren't coming easily. I still have a couple of weeks to go before I'm done with this first draft, so by the time you read this, I doubt I'll have any nails left.

That's okay. They *do* grow back--at the rate of one centimeter every 100 days.

CHAPTER TWENTY-FOUR

Christian Writer . . . or Writer Who's a Christian?

JERRY FALWELL WAS THE FIRST PERSON TO ASK ME THAT question, and he caught me unprepared. We were doing a televised interview, and I might have sat still and blinked for a moment as I considered his question. I was a new writer in those days, and I hadn't really thought about the difference between a Christian writer and a writer who was a Christian. When he asked that question, however, I realized he'd hit upon something I needed to consider.

Was I someone who would write for Christians or a Christian writer who would write for anyone?

For me, the answer has always been the latter. Maybe it's the fact that I grew up in public schools as a child, or maybe it's just a particular call God has on my life. But even though most of my books have been published by Christian publishers and read by Christians, I've never seen Christians as my primary target.

With a few exceptions.

Let me explain. My first book, a picture book, won a contest sponsored by Abingdon Press, a Methodist publishing house. The prize was created to honor Lorna Balian, one of their authors, so before I started writing I went to the library to check out some of her books. I found them to be warm and delightful, but they were not overtly Christian.

So I came up with a story in the same mold—warm, humorous, and fun, but not explicitly Christian. The book won the contest and was published—and no one was more surprised than I was.

Later the editor explained that Abingdon was attempting to launch a new line of books that would be based on Christian values but would still appeal to libraries and general market bookstores. My second book was all set to go when the company pulled the line entirely, so both of my books—the first and the unpublished second—quietly went away. I learned a lot about the realities of the publishing life in only a few short months.

In the mean time, I wrote a couple of nonfiction books that have Christian content because I am a Christian. My faith is such a huge part of who I am that it's difficult for me to talk about certain topics without referring to biblical principles. So my books on adoption and middle school age characteristics (my husband is a middle school pastor) were factual, but contained a lot of references to biblical family life.

Then I realized that one of my favorite folk tales, *The Tale of Three Trees,* did not exist in picture book format. I wrote up the story according to the picture book blueprint and made a few changes that were uniquely mine. Lion Publishing bought the story and described it as a "spiritual story for secular people." It is my best-selling book.

I love that book because Jesus's name is never mentioned, so I am free to read it almost anywhere. Yet it is completely about Jesus, of course. It's a parable about people and what happens when people lose faith in God because their plans are frustrated.

Over the years, I took a hard look at the stories Jesus told. And I realized that rarely did his stories ever have an obvious religious component—he wrote of farmers and fathers and housewives and weddings, of shepherds and fools, the rich and the poor. Yes, his stories had deep spiritual meanings, but not everyone caught them. Jesus went on to say that not everyone was *meant* to catch them.

His disciples came and asked him, "Why do you use parables when you talk to the people?"

He replied, "You are permitted to understand the secrets of the Kingdom of Heaven, but others are not. To those who listen to my teaching, more understanding will be given, and they will have an abundance of knowledge. But for those who are not listening, even what little understanding they have will be taken away from them. That is why I use these parables,

For they look, but they don't really see. They hear, but they don't really listen or understand (Matthew 13:10-13, NLT).

Over the years, I have worked hard to write parables for the world. And lest my book ignite a spiritual spark that leads someone off in the wrong direction, I include discussion questions at the end to gently lead them toward the biblical truth I've written about.

I think of my stories as onions—there's an outer story that should be entertaining and appealing, but there are inner layers as well. Those only serve to deepen the richness, meaning, and theme of the story.

A few of my books have been written specifically for Christians—*The Debt* springs immediately to mind—and I don't expect secular people to understand the full meaning of that book. In an age when people are increasingly offended by any mention of Jesus Christ, my parable stories do not use a lot of religious jargon. The entire time I'm writing, I struggle to break out of my religious habits and write in a language that ordinary people use.

Of course my Christian worldview is present in my books—I

could no more break out of that than I could lose thirty pounds with the wave of a magic wand. I do write for Christians, but I am aiming for the world. They may not always understand the deeper messages in my books, but I'm not responsible for making them understand. The Holy Spirit is the One who brings understanding in His perfect time.

Some of my Christian brothers and sisters call themselves "Christian writers" and they write for Christians because Christians certainly need edifying literature. I applaud their efforts and I enjoy their books.

But God gives us tasks that fit our personalities and our gifts, and the task he's given me is to write all kinds of books that celebrate life and love and humor and joy and children and animals and all that God has given us. And that is what I aim to do.

I remember a few years ago when Amy Grant recorded an album of mostly secular songs—some Christians carried on as if she'd renounced her salvation entirely. That position is not only unreasonable, it's illogical. Should a Christian dentist work only on Christian teeth? Should a Christian plumber work only on Christians' pipes?

Years ago Christians pulled out of the movie industry, and movies have gone downhill ever since. We must not relegate ourselves and our art to Christian ghettoes. We must continue to write and create and sing and work with excellence, and we must take our rightful place in the world in which God has placed us.

In the upper room on the night before his crucifixion, Jesus prayed, "I'm not asking you to take them out of the world, but to keep them safe from the evil one. They do not belong to this world any more than I do. Make them holy by your truth; teach them your word, which is truth. Just as you sent me into the world, I am sending them into the world" (John 17:15-18).

As a Christian writer, you may feel called to write for the church—and that is certainly an appropriate task because believers need books to help them grow in grace, knowledge, and love. Other writers will feel that they have been called to reach the world. Those of us who accept this latter task must cling to the Word of God in order to remain holy and discerning. We need to shine the light of Christ, and not be swallowed up by darkness. And we must ditch the Christianese and speak in a language the world can understand.

I don't know which tasks God will place before you. But I hope you will do them with all your skill, all your might, and all your courage and conviction. Your art should be a holy offering to the Lord, no matter where it is published.

Godspeed, my friend, wherever the Lord leads you!

AFTERWORD

Thank you for purchasing this book in **Writing Lessons from the Front.** If you find any typos in this book, please write and let us know where they are: hunthaven@gmail.com.

We would also appreciate it if you would be kind enough to leave a review of this book on Amazon. Thank you!

If you would like to purchase all of the Writing Lessons from the Front in one book, you may do so here.

ABOUT THE AUTHOR

Angela Hunt writes for readers who have learned to expect the unexpected from this versatile writer. With over four million copies of her books sold worldwide, she is the best-selling author of more than 150 works ranging from picture books (*The Tale of Three Trees*) to novels and nonfiction.

Now that her two children have reached their twenties, Angie and her husband live in Florida with Very Big Dogs (a direct result of watching *Turner and Hooch* too many times). This affinity for mastiffs has not been without its rewards—one of their dogs was featured on *Live with Regis and Kelly* as the second-largest canine in America. Their dog received this dubious honor after an all-expenses-paid trip to Manhattan for the dog and the Hunts, complete with VIP air travel and a stretch limo in which they toured New York City. Afterward, the dog gave out pawtographs at the airport.

Angela admits to being fascinated by animals, medicine, unexplained phenomena, and "just about everything." Books, she says, have always shaped her life— in the fifth grade she learned how to flirt from reading *Gone with the Wind*.

Her books have won the coveted Christy Award, several Angel Awards from Excellence in Media, and the Gold and Silver Medallions from *Foreword Magazine*'s Book of the Year Award. In 2007, her novel *The Note* was featured as a Christmas movie on the Hallmark channel. She recently completed her doctorate in biblical literature and is now finishing her doctorate in Theology.

When she's not home writing, Angie often travels to teach writing workshops at schools and writers' conferences. And to talk about her dogs, of course. Readers may visit her web site at www.angelahuntbooks.com.

For more information:
www.angelahuntbooks.com
Angie@angelaelwellhunt.com

ALSO BY ANGELA HUNT

Esther: Royal Beauty

Bathsheba: Reluctant Beauty

Delilah: Treacherous Beauty

Risen: The Novelization of the Motion Picture

The Offering

The Fine Art of Insincerity

Five Miles South of Peculiar

The Face

Let Darkness Come

The Elevator

The Novelist

The Awakening

The Truth Teller

Unspoken

Uncharted

The Justice

The Canopy

The Immortal

Doesn't She Look Natural?

She Always Wore Red

She's In a Better Place

The Pearl

The Note

The Debt

Then Comes Marriage

The Shadow Women

www.ingramcontent.com/pod-product-compliance
Lightning Source LLC
Chambersburg PA
CBHW071216120626
46546CB00006B/2588